RED YELLOW GREEN

Insights on Dating for Teens

ISAIAH CHRISTIAN JONES

JayMedia Publishing

Printed in the United States of America

First Printing, 2020

JayMedia Publishing

9429 Nicklaus Lane

Laurel, MD 20708

ISBN 978-1-7334432-0-3

Table of Contents

FOREWORD

A young lady, a high school teenager, entered my office one day when I worked outside of the classroom as a Peer Mediation Coordinator. She expressed a desire to talk to me and began by displaying great sadness. Her face and body language clearly showed me someone who was deeply troubled. It was hard for her to keep her head up when she began talking. Our conversation revealed this young lady was intensely remorseful in betraying her mother's trust by choosing to date without her mother's permission. Having her mother find out that she disregarded the designated time frame for her to wait to date, which was sixteen, placed a heavy weight on this young lady because she knew she had betrayed her mother's trust. She was overwhelmed by the grief and shame in seeing her relationship with her mom deteriorate because of an unwise decision that may have seemed right at the time but led to the rupture in her relationship with her mom.

As we talked, it was apparent to me this young lady's relationship with her mother was important to her. It hurt her to know her actions both upset her mother and made it difficult for her to relate to her mom, after being found out, since things were different before making the decision to date without her mother's permission. I reinforced to the young lady how her current feelings of knowing her mom was upset with her and the guilt and shame in seeing how her actions created distance in her relationship with her mom are indicators that the relationship with her mother was important to her. It was important to me, in that moment of listening to the young lady, to actually focus on what was not being said instead of just focusing on the subject of dating, because the young lady's grief and remorse over her actions communicated to me a greater problem than her choice to date. At that moment, it was more important that time was allowed for her to cope with how she was feeling as a result of the choice she had made and help her to see a bigger problem she may not be aware of based on the story she told. It is a story and concern I have since shared with my own two children (19 and 17 respectively at the time of writing this foreword) as well as have passed along to other teens on what it means to be 'ready to date.'

As she gathered herself and demonstrated by her body

language a willingness to receive feedback from what was shared, I asked her to consider another perspective and explaining to me her mother's desire for her to wait until she was sixteen to date. I began first, by helping her to see her mother's willingness and open mindedness to allow her to date by providing her a time frame (age sixteen) so she could do what she desired. I began there, because I needed her to see she had a mother (parent) who was supporting her interests even if her mother may not have necessarily agreed with the idea of her daughter dating. I then shared with her the bigger concern she may not have considered. A concern I would ask everyone who reads this book to consider regarding whether you are ready to date. I suggested to her that the fact that she would disregard her mother's desire to wait until she was sixteen and choose to date without her mother's consent and knowledge demonstrates, by her actions, why she was in fact not ready to date.

Having had numerous conversations with teens, by this time, on the subject of dating, it was not important to me to give my opinion of whether she should be dating or whether I approve of her dating. What concerns me more than the subject of dating, whether one believes they are ready to date or not, is whether the one who thinks they're ready understands what it means to be involved in a relationship and have the maturity to handle the real challenges that come with being in a relationship. By choosing to disregard her mother's position to wait and get involved without her mother's knowledge demonstrated actions that indicated not being ready for the responsibility that comes with being in a relationship. I explained to the young lady, who by this time had sat up in her chair and displayed a body language intrigued by what I was communicating, that her actions of betrayal of her mother's trust and disregard for her mother's request to wait validated indirectly that she was not ready. I reminded the young lady her mother's willingness to consider dating as an option when she gets older shows why waiting would be a good decision. If your parents told you to wait until you were 16 what would you do differently than this young lady while you waited to show or demonstrate being 'ready to date?'

I encouraged the young lady to consider repairing the ruptured relationship between her and her mother by admitting her fault, apologizing, and demonstrating patience to wait as her mother suggested. As I have shared with other teens, talking about the subject of dating with their parents requires them to elevate their conversation to the level of concerns adults have about the subject if they truly desire to get their parent's support or approval to date. Parents also need to be able to meet their children where they are in the conversation to build a healthy level of communication on difficult subjects like dating so teens can feel more comfortable to come forward to address other things like thoughts of suicide, bullying, insecurities, feeling angry, depressed, etc. When you mention the desire to 'go to the movies with a friend of the opposite sex', your parents begin to think about sex, pregnancy, kissing, things they would prefer not to think about regarding their children. Even if those things are not on the child's mind, it doesn't mean that parents shouldn't be thinking about it. A parent who loves their child will not willingly expose them to circumstances that can bring ruin into their lives. So, if the desire is to get parental approval, the child must learn to communicate with the parent on their level of concern, without disregarding it as insignificant, or talking about the subject of dating will be difficult.

The concerns parents have about the subject of dating are both real and legitimate regardless of whether the teen thinks or believes them to be or not. Teens who disregard a parent's concerns do so foolishly and unwisely. In my talks with my children and their mother, I have mentioned to them that God would use words like death, destruction, harm, and ruin as outcomes of not taking heed to the wisdom He provides in His word. So thinking that parents are over exaggerating the possible outcomes of engaging in dating is not a helpful perspective to have if a teenager is seeking parent's support or approval to date. As I have shared with my own children, along with other teens, adults also struggle with dating and relationships, so teens should not think they would be immune or escape the real challenges involving dating and relationships. Learning to have healthy open dialogue with your parents about the subject before getting involved will do three important things: 1) strengthen their relationship with their parents, 2) strengthen their ability to communicate about tough topics, and 3) help them be more thoughtful, wise, and informed about decision making and problem solving as they transition into adulthood. Having their parent's support and being able to communicate with them as they're growing up creates more security, confidence, and assurance in themselves while minimizing the amount of times they rely on their feelings to make important decisions involving peer relationships.

Having intense feelings and thoughts is not the problem when it comes to dating and peer relationships, but if a person is not aware they are a part of being in a relationship or how to effectively manage their thoughts and feelings it can harm them to be in a relationship. One day I asked my daughter, "Would you give a knife to a baby to play with?" She responded with an emphatic "No," but wasn't quite sure why I would ask the question. I explained to her that a knife obviously is not a toy, something to play with, and neither is it appropriate to give it to a baby. Dating, to me, is not something a teen should enter into like one would play games. The real harm that can come from getting too involved mentally and emotionally without having an understanding of the impact it can have if they are unprepared to manage what they're thinking and feeling along with having to deal with another person's thoughts and emotions. Way too often, observing the reality of what teens face or encounter growing up, I have heard many stories of male and female youth. Stories such as being overcome by the emotions and thoughts involving dating relationships that ultimately lead to low self-esteem, fractured peer relationships, ruptured parent relationships, poor academic performance, unplanned pregnancies, being distracted and driven by emotion in decision making, depression, emotional trauma, and thoughts leading to self-harm and suicide.

I recall a young lady in high school coming to talk with me upset with her mother giving her the ultimatum to choose between remaining at home or remaining in a relationship with her boyfriend. The young lady was upset that she would have to choose and was seriously considering her relationship with her boyfriend over living at home. I also recall within that same school community, a young lady who acknowledged understanding the need to end what was unfolding as an unhealthy relationship, but needing to understand how to do it. I recall two young men who were having a tough time emotionally with the reality that their relationships were ending and struggling to process how they were feeling and being able to recover and move on. These are just some of the realities I have had the privilege of being made aware of, as students would come forward to confide in me about the challenges associated with dating. Lack of parental communication, guidance, support, being unprepared in coping with the real challenges associated with what relationships involve and when they end, and not having a healthy sense of self that allows teens to thrive and still have high self-esteem after a relationship ends are important concepts teens need to be aware of in regards to dating. However, most won't learn in isolation operating in secrecy without parental involvement and communication.

I also recall a young lady who took my advice, while in middle school, to initiate conversation with her parents to include them in her desire and interest to date. I had the privilege of learning from her, upon her graduation from high school, that the talks with her mom over the years aided her in navigating the challenges surrounding dating as she grew into her adulthood. She said every step of the way wasn't rainbows and unicorns, but believed the initiative and effort to talk was a huge help in her journey into adulthood. She cited that those talks also enabled her to maintain her virginity throughout high school. She has since graduated from college, has gotten married, and is now thriving in life as an adult. She also has the support of family and a healthy sense of self intact. I credit her efforts to keep her parents involved in those critical life decisions growing up as she transitioned from being a teenager into becoming an adult. In everything, I observed watching teens date and receiving this young lady's feedback on accepting my advice to involve her parents motivated me to operate with my two children in the same way.

I believe asking for help is an important life skill needed in order to experience a fulfilling and rewarding life. I explained to my two children and the students I teach, that learning to ask for help is an important life skill, even for adults. Being an adult doesn't mean you won't ever need to ask for help. Teens, who can develop an ability to have tough conversations with their parents about tough topics, while learning to ask for help in tense, difficult circumstances, will transition well into adulthood with a healthy self-esteem intact. I explained to my son and daughter when we seek to operate in life without help from God, through prayer, we are telling God that we can handle the thoughts and feelings we encounter and the circumstances we face. When teens operate in isolation, independent of their parents without support, guidance, or advice, they do so more often to their own harm. Talking with their parents enables teens to think critically and prepare to make decisions, apart from how they feel, that can spare them unnecessary hardship, trauma, and difficulties learned from poor decision making. There are some life lessons that can be understood without having to experience the difficult negative outcomes resulting from poor decision-making.

How does it feel trying to manage all those thoughts and emotions on your own without asking for help, guidance, or input from trusted adults or God?

I am excited for you to be reading my son Isaiah's book on teen dating. When he read another book titled *Dateable,* he shared with me insights he had learned from reading it. I encouraged him to put in a book of his own to help others as the book *Dateable* did for him. I was invited to read that book by a high school student and immediately began sharing it with other high school students. In all my years of experience in talking with teens on the subject of dating, I would ask any young person to consider "How good are you feeling about who you are?" If their motivation to date is in any way driven by making them feel good about who they are, feeling like having this title will validate who they are or their attractiveness, or because everyone else is, then I would encourage them to stop and think critically about the desire and decision to date. A healthy self-esteem has more to do with what is said and done to make someone feel good about who they are. This can be achieved by putting more time and energy in working hard at school, investing time in your interests related to dancing, writing, drawing, singing, etc., and journaling your thoughts and feelings to take inventory about what's going on inside. The biggest mistake I've seen made by teens in dating is the amount of time they invest emotionally, physically, and in time with others, while struggling academically and in discovering more about who they are and their future life goals. My advice to my children included not making desires and interests in dating more important than their life goals such as graduating from high school, going to college, pursuing a career, purchasing a home, learning to take care of yourself, etc. My children having a healthy sense of self without feeling they needed to date to be secure, confident, and assured in who they are was important to me as a parent.

I hope you enjoy the content of this book written by my son Isaiah, who has a sincere heart with an interest in working with and helping youth. I believe if you read this book with an open heart and open mind you will find help to provide you guidance, direction, and support on the subject of teen dating. I also believe, if you are willing to accept the challenge of learning to engage in healthy, open communication with your parents and working through the challenges of doing it, you will not regret it.

Cortland Jones

INTRODUCTION

WHEN I was in middle school, probably in 7th grade, I met this girl named Jordan. Man, I thought she was cute and we were friends. Little did I know that she liked me so I was pumped up. I had just gotten braces and a new haircut that summer so I was very confident in myself. In middle school, I shared an iPhone with my sister, so I would beg her to use it. My girlfriend and I would text but nothing serious happened until she said she wanted to be my girlfriend. I had no idea what a girlfriend really was but me being thirteen and a girl liking me, I was all in! We started "dating" in 7th grade and I was a happy camper; her friends, not so much. They didn't like me for whatever reason. But I didn't let that phase me, I had a girlfriend. Well that didn't last long because I told my sister and my sister told my mom. My mom made me break up with her - my first GIRLFRIEND! The next day at school, I was sad and scared I would hurt her telling her "I'm breaking up with you" so I told her friend. Her friend told her other friends, who eventually told my girlfriend. Crazy right! I thought I was gonna be okay telling her friend but nope wrong idea.

My girlfriend blew up my phone that day after school and when I called her to tell her the news she wasn't mad because she understood that I wasn't allowed to date. My parents told me I was not allowed to start dating until I was 16 years old. I never knew why at that age but I didn't care. I thought it was dumb to wait so I continued trying to date. That summer my dad took my sister and me to Ocean City and we started reading a book called *Dateable*. In my mind I'm thinking *Why read a book about something that I can figure out on my own* and I thought, *This is dumb, I don't want to do this*. My dad said, "You finish this book, you can date!"

So you would think I finished the book by the end of the summer, right? WRONG! It took me four YEARS to read that book! FOUR YEARS! In my mind in those four years, I didn't think that book was important, I actually lost the book in my room! In those four years, I had a couple of "relationships" trying to figure out this game we called dating. Until these two girls I dated. The first one was a rollercoaster. I met her on Instagram and started following her because I thought she was cute. Little did I know she had just gotten out of a relationship. She DM'd me saying, "Hi" and I said, "Hey wassup!" We talked a bit and she thought I was cute. So I was thinking *Okay I'm in there, let me get to know this girl.* Little did I know, she had a bad reputation in school for being an easy girl. But I did not care, I was attracted to the girl I wanted and she liked me too. We talked every day and I thought I was "in love."

Fast forward a couple weeks and I would send her heart emojis, I love you texts, liking all her Instagram posts, doing what I thought was okay. I was in 10th grade, I wasn't mature yet so I did cringy and dumb things. One night at dinner with my dad and sister, my dad said, "Who's your girlfriend?" I was shocked, literally speechless because I thought he didn't know I was dating. I was fifteen so I couldn't date and I didn't read that book so I definitely couldn't date. So my fifteen year old self told him, "She's just a friend." He wasn't buying it so I came clean after lying to him about my girlfriend and he said, "Break up with her, you aren't allowed to date." But me being secretive I didn't do it, I stayed with her. Two or three months later, he caught me lying again, sat down, and had a talk with me. He brought up the book and asked "Have you read your book?" and I said, "No". We read the first chapter in the car and he said, "Break up with that girl." So I did. I sent a text saying, "I'm breaking up with you, I'm not allowed to date." She called me crying, asking "Why?" and saying, "Don't do this, I love you."

She told her mom we were breaking up and her mom texted me and said, "Stay with my daughter keep her happy." At that point I was done. When we were over a few days later, she started another relationship and I started reading my book. Both didn't last long. She was in numerous relationships and I stopped reading my book. I figured I'd give up on dating because it wasn't worth it. It wasn't worth reading about because I didn't think the book would help.

Fast forward to the summer of 2018 and I was working as a tech guy for my step dad's company, MSI, and we had a job doing sound for a week long church conference. They were daylong shifts so I had lots of time. I talked to my stepdad about the book and he told me, "You won't be able to go anywhere until you read that book." So I owned up to it and read the book. I read half of it in five days and the other half in the two weeks after that. I didn't just read the book; I fell in love with it. So much that I started spreading my new knowledge to some of my peers. I learned so much from reading that book that I could see in real life what I was learning.

Later that summer in August, I met this girl at my week

long NJROTC camp. I was sixteen and finished my book so I was thinking I could finally date now. This young lady and I became buddies during the camp and on Thursday, she told me she liked me. I was friends with her sister so I thought *Okay; I'll give her a chance.* Immediately, we clicked and it took off from there. The funny thing was that she couldn't date until she was sixteen. I ended up taking this girl to homecoming and meeting her parents. That was the most stressful day of my life up to that point because I wanted to make a good impression. The young lady's father and mother asked me lots of questions that I wasn't prepared for, but there was one question her dad asked that stuck with me. The question was "What do you want to do when you grow up?" And I said, "I want to help change the world." I had no idea what that meant but I thought it would make sense. At the end of the day, he ended up really liking me and I went back for Thanksgiving while I dated this girl.

We dated for three months before I called it quits. Those three months were up and down; every day was a new challenge I wasn't ready for. Even before dating, I was presented with challenges I didn't think I could face. But I prayed a lot. After three months of wishy- washy emotions, lack of trust and communication, my heart, mind and soul couldn't take it. I was, on most nights, broken hearted and had lots of anxiety or I was mad and upset. Emotionally, I was at my lowest and I wasn't the same. I didn't include my parents in this and this affected our relationship. Also my friend noticed I wasn't in the best place either. So much so he told me to leave her because I was not happy and it was a toxic relationship. So I left her, she was upset but it was time and I felt much better.

Dating isn't easy, trust me I know. Even if you think you're ready, you're not. I'm almost an adult and I'm not ready; so children in middle school definitely aren't ready, and their parents would agree. My dad told me, "If you can't take care of yourself, how will you take care of someone else?" That makes perfect sense because you won't succeed in a relationship if you aren't 100%. Nothing will work, so don't try it. I think teens are ready to date when:

a. They have a car,

b. They have a job, and

c. They have their parents' approval

You need all three to date, most parents will agree. I know my parents would not let me date until I read the book *Dateable*. It's the best book I've ever read because it was a book that made me learn more about myself before dating. If you have a car, job and parents approval, dating will be fun. First, if you have your own car, you can go anywhere. Second, if you have a job, you have an income, you have your own money and won't you have to ask your parents for money. Third, a parent's approval and trust is the best thing ever. You get to have fun just don't do too much.

I want to write this book because teens aren't ready to be in the dating stage yet. It's way too soon, we think with our emotions more than our brains as teens. Mentally and emotionally, you aren't ready to take care of yourself let alone another human being.

If you think you're ready and you don't have those three things you're wrong. You're not ready unless you have involved your parents in some type of way. If you don't then you will be experiencing all the negatives in a relationship on your own, and all the bad days or arguments that you have with your girlfriend or boyfriend you will have to deal with alone. Emotionally and mentally, it impacts you negatively because you hold in emotions. If you have no outlets then you self-implode. God is the best and most valuable option to have besides your parents. If you desire not to tell them, since one of God's commandments is to honor your parents, then you are going behind their backs and you're not honoring them.

Lastly, I want to help you. My teacher always says

help me, help you. I want kids to know that they aren't ready to date. Ready meaning, mature, being financially stable (having a job) and having transportation (your own car) because not all parents are willing to be your ride. You also have to be respectful and responsible because if you don't respect your parents or don't take care of school or chores, you're not ready to date. Kids nowadays do not open up to their parents and they start dating behind their parents' backs. Then there's a lot of heartbreak and secrecy that goes unresolved because everyone wants to do what they want & when they want. Social media has opened up a gateway to be sneaky because most parents don't think to check. This generation needs to know if they are ready to date or not because it will affect the next one. So help me help you and let me explain my thoughts on teen dating.

RED LIGHT

A Male Perspective

Red Light definition:

Stop the relationship if:

1. You are attracted to the boy/girl just because of looks/physical attraction.

2. Your parents don't approve of the boy/girl.

3. It has a lot of drama or negative energy.

4. If you're just in it for sexual pleasure.

AS we get older, we are taught, "not to judge a book by its cover." Yeah, in elementary school, the saying is meant to be about actual books but as we grow teens, it is meant to be about our peers. It was about friendship at first but then it turned to dating. When I was in fifth grade, I remember walking up to two girls at my school and asking if I could be friends and sit with them. They said, "Eww, no you can't." In elementary school, I had gaps in my teeth and wasn't really confident in myself. I never really had a lot of friends, and I was bullied in elementary school because of my teeth. I remember a girl telling me she would not date me because I had gaps in my teeth. I never really let that stop me from going out there and making friends. In the summer before 7th grade, I got my braces. Immediately, I got more attention from people and the girls came in hot. I remember I had three girlfriends that year because I was more confident in myself. I had more friends because I opened myself up because of my confidence. I think as I went through puberty, I was unsure of my outcome.

You're probably thinking, Isaiah what does that have to do with teen dating? You have to love yourself first before you love anyone else, either as friends or in a relationship. You have to have self-love and value yourself. I've met many teens who have trouble loving themselves so they don't treat others well. That happens in relationships. I have friends whose girlfriends or boyfriends didn't love themselves and took it out on the other person. That's not healthy in a relationship or in a friendship. I had a friend who was insecure about herself so she never opened up in a relationship and then was upset when her boyfriend would break up with her. You need to open up and communicate with your boy/girlfriend about your insecurities.

On the other end of the spectrum, there are people out here basing their relationships off of outside looks. I don't think this is a healthy way to choose your boy/girlfriend because relationships don't work because of how cute the couple is. It works with communication and comprehension from both sides to find common ground. I never thought of dating a girl because of her body. If someone's personality isn't that good then I don't want to get to know them. If their personality is amazing then I'm instantly attracted and if they have a good looking body then it's an add on. A girl's body isn't the first priority. I remember I was in sixth grade; there was this Latina young lady in my class. All the boys were trying to get to know her because her body was more developed than the other girls were. She and I ended up becoming good friends, partially because I liked her but mainly because I wasn't trying super hard to get with her. She ended up in a relationship with this guy so everyone stopped trying.

That's a perfect example of what not to do. Don't chase after a girl for their body, you should get to know the girl and be friends with her first. Don't be the guy trying super hard to get her because in the process you never really get anywhere. The guys who get the girls are the guys that are either really confident and get them on the spot or they take their time and they get to know them. Don't waste your time trying to get the cutest girl in the group, especially if they have no substance. It reminds me of the movie, *Mean Girls*, because all those pretty girls were mean. Why go after a pretty girl if she's mean? Go after a girl with substance and personality, I bet you it'll be worth your time.

Girls out there, if you know guys are chasing you because you look good, be selective of who you pick. Not all guys have good motives, some guys like to hit and quit, some guys wanna make you theirs but can't keep a steady relationship and others want to show you a good time. It's your decision to choose wisely because if you pick the first two options, you're in for a roller coaster ride. Just like how I said guys need to pick a girl with substance, girls need to do the same. I've seen it happen many, many, many times with my closest female friends. I knew a girl who liked this guy, he claimed he liked her back but then played her for about a month thinking they would date. I know another girl who got into a relationship with a guy for five months and he lied to her the entire time. We all make mistakes when we pick people to date but we all get a lesson afterwards. No one is perfect, including me. I was set up with this girl by my best friend and I thought, *Yeah I could make this work*. I didn't know the girl very well but I figured I could get to know her and before I knew it, me and her had chemistry quickly. But I made a poor decision and got physically involved way too quick.

We were physically involved with each other for four days before I told her I wanted to slow things down. It went downhill after that because she wasn't comprehending what I was communicating. The whole weekend was a constant back and forth about her feelings and that next week she showed them to me. When we had school she was very clingy and wouldn't leave me alone. The next day we didn't talk because I told her I needed space. The next day she ranted to the whole school about me. I ended up telling her we couldn't talk anymore and she got upset and told me to never talk to her again.

One reason I didn't want to date her was because I was writing this book. She didn't understand I had goals I was chasing and she wasn't one of those goals. She was upset I put things ahead of her instead of making her number one. To everyone reading this book, put your goals first. No boy or girl is worth you not reaching your potential. She kept telling me I was putting her off because I was busy with other things, which was true. Young women and men don't be afraid to chase your dreams. Girls and guys will come for a long time but your goals and dreams are hard to obtain after a period of time.

Another reason I didn't want her was because she was a smoker. First off, all my friends know I don't like smokers or wouldn't date one at least. I caught her smoking and she thought I was overreacting when it's not attractive to me. She was killing her chances with me. If you have someone in your life who is killing their chances with you then don't allow them to think they have a chance because they don't. You are too valuable as a person to pity date someone, enjoy your life.

Last thing she kept my name in drama. Drama is not healthy in a relationship or in life in general. She said if she had sex with me she could keep me. Two things are wrong with that equation: 1) I didn't want to have sex with her and, 2) I wasn't going to stay just because we were having sex. Don't stay with someone for sex, you are too young to be making those types of bold and grown choices. You need to know when you're getting into a toxic relationship. Some signs you will be able to tell because you have boundaries. Boundaries are things you set in place to protect you. Trust me we all need them, it's the key to a healthy relationship. Boundaries will help you see red flags and that's very important for the red light.

The last two things I want to share are parents' approval and God's approval. These two are major in the dating world because it heavily affects the way you participate in relationships. Let me explain!

When your parents allow you to date, they want you to be in a valuable relationship. They don't want you running around with these girls or guys who don't have any substance. They are looking out for you because they want the best for you! They know way more than you think.

Parents have been around the block and they might have done things that you can learn from. Just ask them or talk to them. Not only will you learn but you have built a stronger connection with them because you are opening up. When I opened up with my mom, our relationship became stronger. It takes time but it also takes courage.

Last, but definitely not least, God is very important in the dating world. In the bible, it never talks about dating, but the bible does talk about not having sex before marriage. This is important because so many teens want to have sex and it's not right. God sees everyone as single until you become married. Your relationship will work better if you're a Christian and you date someone who is also a Christian because then you see eye to eye. I personally feel like God guides you when you're trying to get into a relationship. While writing this book I was tempted with relationships as time takers. Now, I'm not perfect, I fell into temptation but then God will show or will tell me things to get back on track because I was doing something He gave me time to accomplish. Listen to God because He loves you and wants you to do great things.

RED LIGHT

A Female Perspective

As young women, whether we are teens or young adults, we eventually want to be in a relationship with someone. It's only natural to be with someone that you like a lot, or at least you may think you like a lot.

A lot of young women feel three things about being in relationship:

- They want to be with a guy because they have genuine feelings towards them

- They're bored and want to be entertained

- They see girls they know in relationships and suddenly want to be in one also

It is important to know your motives for wanting to get in a relationship in the first place because that is the determining factor on if you're ready to be in a relationship and how long it will last. It also can be a look into the decisions or possible mistakes you tend to make while in a relationship.

These are three major signs that you need to look out for when getting involved in a relationship. Some decisions/mistakes often made by young women can be:

- Putting boyfriend over life priorities
- Rushing into a relationship or rushing while in the relationship
- Keeping secrets from parents

When getting into a relationship your priorities or goals should be number one. A boyfriend/girlfriend should not distract you from your work, goals, or other important things you have going on in life. If you have placed your significant other higher than your priorities, then things will not work out. You will then begin to see that 1) your partner won't do the same for you, or 2) both of you will place each other before your priorities. Both of you should complement each other with each person doing their own thing on their own time without the other interfering. If you are seeing that maybe you don't have enough time to handle a boyfriend/girlfriend or you don't see separating your priorities and relationship as something important, then maybe a relationship is not for you right now.

There really isn't a time frame of when a relationship should start or when the perfect time is to start certain things within the relationship. In this time period, we as a generation have this thing called the "talking stage", and this is a stage that many young adults either don't understand or don't see the reason for it. The talking stage is something that many people have different definitions of which makes it the confused term it is today. It's the equivalent to dating. The time where you get to feel out the person you are interested in for an amount of time, or even feeling out multiple people depending on how you date. No one should be in a solid relationship within the span of one month, and if you are then I guarantee the relationship has slim chances of lasting long. Also, when you both are together, make sure you are both on the same page. Young couples tend to move fast in relationships when it comes to commitment, sex, or even how they feel. I'm not here to tell you what you should do in your relationship because that's your business, but I am here to encourage smart thinking when it comes to a healthy relationship. When you are young, commitment is something that shouldn't cross your mind because you're not getting married. Loyalty should be a major key, not commitment. Sex should not be the focus of the relationship, but if you decide to be sexually active, sexual relations should be an agreement when BOTH are on the same page. Often times sex is pushed more from one than the other and you both should be comfortable. If your boyfriend really wants to have sex and you're not comfortable with taking that step yet then let him know. If he has a problem with it then maybe he's not someone you need to be in a relationship with. The moment you become sexually active your chances of becoming pregnant increases and that can have an impact on you, your family, future goals and the child. A dating relationship that involves sex as a teenager is a dangerous relationship because it intensifies the challenges involving your thoughts, emotions, and decision making that makes having a healthy dating relationship less possible as a teenager.

When it comes to relationships and dating, it's important to include your parents in your relationship. No, that doesn't mean include your parents in all of your relationships' business, but it means inform them that you're in some type of relationship. I say this because many teens make the mistake of not including their parents thinking they can do dating by themselves, when in reality they can't. Your parents can give you wisdom and advice that you don't have because they've been in your shoes before and probably experienced some of the things you're experiencing right now.

The red light is important when it comes to relationships and dating. It shows what you need to stop and evaluate when you decide to get involved in a relationship. In this generation relationships are showcased everywhere from social media, music, tv shows, movies, and media. There are even books on how relationships are supposed to be. It's important for you to realize why you want a relationship and to be smart about the decisions you make while dating.

QUESTIONS FOR TEENS TO THINK ABOUT

- Use the notes section to answer and think critically about what you're reading

- Think about a question(s) you would want to ask your parent(s) or trusted adult

1. Why is it important to take time to learn more about yourself before getting involved in dating relationships?

2. Why would talking with your parents or a trusted adult be helpful before you begin dating?

3. Why should you be cautious about dating without parental approval, support, or guidance?

4. What's wrong with dating someone that you are only attracted to physically?

5. What about reading the Red Light section stood out to you?

6. If you are already dating, why is it important to stop and evaluate where you are, how you're feeling, and whether this relationship is healthy?

7. Do you think sex makes a relationship better, prevents the relationship from ending, or motivates the other person to remain committed and faithful to the relationship?

8. Is your only reason or motivation for dating because everyone else is or do you feel left out, bored, alone, or insecure about yourself and think a relationship will solve those feelings?

9. Why would a dating relationship not solve those feelings or is it possible to experience those feelings while you are dating?

10. If dating doesn't resolve those feelings, then what should you do if any of those feelings (or feelings in general) is what's motivating your desire to date?

Notes

YELLOW LIGHT

A Male Perspective

Yellow Light definition:

1. Think about whether this person is someone you would want to take home to meet family/take out.

2. Check to make sure you really like this person before you commit seriously to spending time with them and to avoid being driven by and acting on your emotions.

3. Since teenagers act on emotion, don't let emotions and lust drive the decision making involving your dating life.

THIS light is that in between space between red and green light and this light is important. This is a time period where you are learning about who you are or who the other person is. If you are learning who you are, take your time and it's the same if you are learning about someone else. Learning who you are means asking yourself questions, learning your hobbies, the way you work in and out of school, and other things in the future. If you don't know what you're going to do with your life, you need to know because it's important. I remember I didn't know what I wanted to do with my life and I kept getting involved with girls for no reason. My dad would always tell me colleges won't ask how many girlfriends I had in high school because it doesn't matter. You have to be able to be okay with being alone or by yourself being single. Alone time is the best time. Alone time = Single life! There is nothing wrong with being single. After going through life being single it's helped me a lot. I used to be sad and lonely but God gives you time to be alone and you need to take advantage of it instead of wasting it. While being single I used that time to write this book. Being single allows me time and opportunity to do things to enhance who I am that being in a relationship may distract me from doing. To prepare me for my future or simply in learning to enjoy being a teenager.

When I was in middle school, I wasted so much time! Three straight years I didn't use my time to do the things

I wanted to do, such as accomplish my goals. My goal going into ninth grade was to play high school basketball. I never fulfilled that dream because I was messing around with girls and not getting other goals completed, such as honor roll or getting my permit.

This is one reason why your parents don't want you to date. You have a list of things in 7th grade through 12th grade that needs to be done.

Just to name a couple:

- 8th grade graduation
- PSAT study
- Prepare for high school graduation
- Learner's permit for driver's license
- Prepare for getting a job or pursuing your career after high school
- Take ACT & SAT test (and doing well on it)
- Maintain Honor Roll or higher
- Participate in Youth Service for Church
- Prepare for college

Girlfriends and boyfriends are not important in your teen years. Yes, I know it's fun and you "gotta" have one but they aren't anything but friends you kiss and time consumers. If you have a girlfriend or boyfriend that doesn't take up your time because they are doing the same things on that list then I'm happy for you but you're not really in a relationship then. The point I'm trying to make is, it's easier to do those things when you're single. I tried doing those things while I was in relationships and it doesn't work because most times someone feels like they aren't getting the attention they "deserve" which is funny to me because no one deserves that type of attention but God. If you put the time you're spending in "relation-ships" and switch it and put it in God you'll see your life get easier. It's important to keep an interaction with God while you're single because He helps you achieve your biggest dreams & goals. God wants to see you win and so do your parents.

There were many times I talked to girls just for fun. I never really had a plan after I got them. Having a plan in a relationship means having a map for how far you want to go. If you don't have a plan, your relationship won't go far. I didn't have a plan with my ex so I now understand why we didn't work. With my ex at first, I noticed things in our relationship that were off. I got many red flags but I stayed because I felt like she would mature with me but that didn't happen. I learned that not everyone is willing to change to keep a relationship going. People will only go but so far so don't overextend yourself trying to save a dying relationship.

Some of the things she did included constantly going to social media to vent and have a lot of guys intervening in our relationship. It wasn't that I didn't like her because I did but I stayed way too long just to make her happy even when I wasn't. We would constantly fight and disagree or she would be too moody for me. I know I did things wrong but at some point you have to know when a relationship is toxic and get out of it. At this particular time in life I wasn't my best self so I started to look to her to make me happy, which was not a good idea. She couldn't make me happy all the time because that's my job. In this relationship, we were in between red and yellow light, which was not good at all. We broke up because I personally couldn't deal with it. That relationship wasn't good for me at the time.

Being in a relationship is hard but being in one with someone who's not mature is a different ball game. If you both can't communicate or share your feelings with each other without fighting or breaking up then you can't be in that relationship. If you can't be honest with your girlfriend or boyfriend then you should reconsider your relationship because you are not communicating. There is a difference between electronic communication and face-to-face communication in a relationship. Electronic communication such as texting and FaceTime won't allow you to see the other person's full body language or sense their mood. Face to face communication must be a given in a relationship because of how important it is. It's important to see how the other person reacts, their body language and mood because those things will affect a relationship. If you all don't talk about the problems, issues, good and bad then your relationship will become stale and unfulfilling.

Another thing you need to think about is if the boy/girl you like is someone you could take home. You have to think about whether your family would like the young woman or young man. If they wouldn't then don't even think about taking them home or to family events. I remember I met a young lady's parents and they liked me then I met her extended family and they liked me as well. The bad thing about it was that our relationship didn't last so I had to stop seeing them. Her family still wants the best for me as a person but if you aren't committed or you aren't planning on staying together, don't meet each other's extended family.

One thing you should not do in this stage is act on emotion. That's one of the worst things to do because you don't know where they could take you in the long run.

Say you like someone, they're super attractive, and they like you too. STOP THERE! Don't try to make a relationship out of it too fast or you'll be back in the red light. You gotta settle down first, be friends for some time then engage in the idea of a relationship but only if you are allowed to date. You have to know basic things about the person before you date them.

First you need to think about whether the person you like is someone you would want to take home. If it's not because of personal reasons you know of then don't try to make it a goal to date someone your parents won't approve of. Trust me and take it from me that won't work with parents. My mom told me I couldn't date certain girls. I never really understood why because at my school there were certain girls I was attracted to and the other girls that weren't really my type. I was so pressed to date certain girls just because I felt those were my only options. I never thought about dating girls who attended other schools because I knew I would never see them. Knowing my mom wouldn't let me date certain girls made me upset because I felt like I couldn't have a girlfriend. I talked to her any time I could about it but I never could change her mind. She didn't want me getting hurt and having lifelong effects just because of one girl. I'm happy she never changed her mind because I wouldn't have grown in my thinking about having an interest in other girls. You have to think about what you're looking for in a guy or a girl.

- Don't pursue a relationship just because your friends are doing it. You need to be prioritized with school and have a connection with your family and with God.

- Before you start dating, you need to be clear on what your priorities are in life. When you're not clear on your priorities then life gets confusing.

- Does the person you have an interest in communicate with you about their thoughts, feelings, interest, etc. If they don't, how do you know you are on the same page?

- Are you in a relationship right now? If so, are you genuinely happy? If you aren't, then you need to leave the relationship because you're the one in charge of your own thoughts and emotions. The other person's job isn't to make you happy, you should already feel that way and if you don't you should leave the relationship.

- Meeting the parents is important because your parents want to know who you are spending time with and they are providing the transportation and the money for you to date.

- You need to observe how the girl or boy you like interacts with others. Are they always flirting and being too friendly with others? Do they engage in positive conversation with you? If they are sad or depressed, help encourage them to get help but don't jump into a relationship because emotionally they aren't ready for that. It takes time to get over the pain so don't rush it. Hurt people, hurt people. Don't get into a relationship trying to help or fix anyone because that won't benefit you. Watch how they handle stressful situations. If they break down mentally and emotionally don't date them. They aren't strong enough to get through those problems yet and it will be more challenging for both of you to be in a relationship.

- The final thought is to consider how you manage your time. There is no problem talking to or texting the girl/guy you like. It all comes down to when school or your home life starts to suffer. School and home life should not suffer because of your desire to date. Time is all you have as a teenager. Don't waste the time you have and use it for the things that will benefit you.

Over the summer, I had a 30-day college orientation workshop, which taught us how to manage our time. Before that one of my father's main life points was time management so while I was at the camp, I could see the relation between the two. While I was at the camp, they taught us little things like how to productively study and do homework in two hours or how to get to class on time. After this workshop, a month later my dad held a workshop explaining how creating a calendar for the month helps you break down time and put it in where you need it most. In all this teaching of time management, I was able to use my skills and write a book. Time management, once you learn how to do it, isn't hard but it does take some effort.

You need to open up to your parents about dating. If they are willing to listen, open up to being willing to listen too, because talking with your parents provides guidance and perspective on the subject of dating in ways teens don't normally think about. Sometimes we are scared to tell our parents things but it's worse to keep secrets. There are some things you need to open up about so your parents will have the ability to check on you. If you don't want to open up to your parents open up to God. He knows what you're dealing with so don't hide from Him. God will still love you no matter what you do.

Yellow Light

A Female Perspective

WE are at the next step ladies - the yellow light. This is where we evaluate what we need to do to become one step closer to being ready for a healthy relationship. You now are with the person you like, but wonder what to do next. Many teens and young adults would jump straight into becoming girlfriend and boyfriend without hesitation, but they're missing many key steps that lead to the healthy relationship that they want.

Some key things to note when taking your next steps are:

- Are we both on the same page?
- Is this someone I would want my parents to meet?

- Do my parents know about them?

- Do I know this person well enough to date them?

These are some things you should consider before you decide to take the next step with the person you're interested in.

When it comes to relationships ladies, we are usually more interested in what goes on than the guys. That's not to say they don't care, but we as females just glorify relationships more than guys. That makes both of you being on the same page much more important. If you want to work towards a relationship, you have to make that known because he may just want sex or maybe he wants the same thing, but you will never know until you have that conversation. I know from personal experience, that when you thoroughly communicate what you want to the other person, it takes all the stress from assuming and it saves time. It also allows both of you to take proper action on what you want. No one wants to be stuck in a situation where someone gets hurt because they wasted their time over improper communication or dishonesty. Consider having the conversation to make sure you're both on the same page because that is a huge step on where you both could possibly end up: going your separate ways or ending up together in a healthy relationship.

Another important thing when it comes to dating is introducing your parents to who you are interested in, especially when you're a teenager. Now, not everyone needs to meet the parents, but your parents should at least be informed. Not every guy makes it to that level of meeting the parents and you have the right to choose when you would like your parents to meet the person you're interested in, even more so when you get older. If you feel that this person is not up to the standard of meeting your parents, then maybe this might not be someone you would want to continue into a relationship with in the future.

Before jumping into a relationship, it's important to know the person you like. Yes, you know who the person is, but do you know much about them? Not just their favorite color or animal, but the morals they follow - things that can tie the relationship together and bring both of you closer. Some people are not an open book and that's okay, but they shouldn't hold out information that's important when it comes to moving forward. You may be a woman that is celibate, so knowing if he follows that moral or not is important to know because it's important to you and maybe you don't need to go into a relationship with him. This is important to consider because even though you may really like this guy, if you both see different views then maybe a relationship is not the best idea.

QUESTIONS FOR TEENS TO THINK ABOUT

- Use the notes section to answer and think critically about what you're reading

- Think about a question(s) you would want to ask your parent(s) or trusted adult

1. If you are a Christian, why should God, along with your parents be included in your decision to date?

2. Why should teens learn to talk with their parents or a trusted adult about teen related issues ?

3. Why should teens not rely solely on what their peers are saying on the subject of teen dating?

4. If adults struggle with dating do you think dating would be any easier as a teenager?

5. If you are currently struggling with managing thoughts, emotions, chores, school, do you think adding the responsibility of dating is a wise decision?

6. How well do you manage your thoughts and emotions currently? **1** real struggle, **2** up and down sometimes, **3** doing okay most days, **4** able to process well, **5** I talk about how I feel, journal, and have parents/adults I confide in

7. Is the person you're dating responsible for making you happy? Why or why not?

8. What should you do if you're dating and not happy in the relationship?

9. If the other person is unhappy, depressed often, demanding a lot of attention, or trying to isolate you away from family and friends what should you do?

10. If the person is critical often, mean in how they communicate, or threatening what should you do?

NOTES

GREEN LIGHT

A Male Perspective

Green Light definition:

1. *Date the person if you both communicate well:* communicating to and comprehending each other helps the relationship remain balanced so it's not one sided. If it's one sided your relationship will not work. Someone will get annoyed and frustrated and end the relationship.

2. *Know what you both want in a relationship:* it's important to know this so that there isn't any confusion. If there is confusion in your relationship then it won't work. That's why you need to communicate.

3. *Your parents approve:* if your parents approve it's easier to date. You now have the privilege to hang out and spend quality time with the person you like. If your parents don't approve then you will not be able to date.

IN the summer of 2019, I met a gentleman named Mr. Pittman. He had talked to my mom about being a potential mentor for me. He was a cool guy and I was excited to work with him. Fast forward to my American freedom presentation in November that I had invited him to, he showed me a picture of his daughter and told me that she went to Huntingtown high school and was on their dance team. I was interested in her when he showed me that picture but I assumed she had a boyfriend because she was really pretty.

Fast forward to November 16, 2019 I had a football tournament for NJROTC and after that, Mr. Pittman took me back to his house to work on a doggie door. On the way there, he told me he would introduce his family to me. He asked if I was nervous or shy and I said no but told me if I wanted to talk to his daughter I'd have to step up and say something first because she was shy. In my mind, I was already nervous because I was going to see her, let alone talk to her. I had put things in my mind like, *She's too pretty to not have a boyfriend* or *What if she thinks I'm weird* or *She won't be attracted to me.* When we stopped at Taco Bell he talked about the last guy she had tried being in a relationship with and how she doesn't like boring guys. So now I'm thinking, "Okay, I know I'm not a boring guy. I'm a pretty fun guy!" Then he explained other reasons why they didn't work out which gave me a confidence boost because we had stuff in common. As we entered his neighborhood, he told me, "I'm not going to help you get with my daughter. If you want her, you have to talk to her." In my mind I'm thinking, *Okay well that shouldn't be too hard right?* I mean, he was basically setting me up to talk to her. This was also a great lesson to learn because if you want a girl all you gotta do is talk to her.

We arrived at his house and we got out of the car. To my surprise, there was this small, cute dog barking on his side of the car and when I walked around the dog jumped up at me. I heard, "Get down Kakes" and then I looked up and saw my mentor's daughter. *She looks better in person than in the picture on the phone,* I thought to myself and then I introduced myself to her. After that, we exchanged numbers, talked for a month and went on a date! Her parents approved and so did mine. I never would have thought that I would be in the position I was in and all I did was say hi. This is what green light is about! Green light is being able to go out, explore, and have fun while making smart decisions. Being able to have freedom is something you want as a teenager. If you don't have it then it seems like you're trapped and you don't want to feel that way because it doesn't feel good at all.

The four main points I want you to get out of this book are: 1) Understand how important communication is, 2) Know what you want in a relationship, 3) Have your parent's permission and last but not least is, 4) Have a healthy relationship with God! If you have and understand these four things on both sides then you should be progressing towards experiencing a healthy dating relationship.

First, I'm going to start with parents' permission because without that I probably wouldn't be writing this book the way I'm writing it. Parents play a big role in our life if you want to believe it or not. My parents will agree that my dating phase took more time than needed because I didn't follow their instructions. When parents stop your dating process or put it on hold it's for your good. If you're reading this book, your parents are helping you become a healthy dater. My parents wouldn't let me date until I was 16 but more importantly not until I read a book. A book that has impacted me in a healthy way. The book that forever changed my life was entitled *Dateable*. The book's basis was to help you improve yourself for dating in the future. If I were you, I would read it.

After I read the book, my parents finally opened up dating to me. It felt good to accomplish a goal that they wanted me to do. We started coming closer as a family unit and I had a better relationship with my mom, after we clashed all the time about dating. Fast forward to now my mom is in full support of it and she gives me permission to take the young lady I like out on dates and go to her house to see her. Your parents aren't being nosey when they ask questions about who you like they only want to know if the person you like will treat you right. They know more than you so it's good to listen so you don't make avoidable mistakes.

Just because you talk to your parents doesn't mean they will let you date. This is where communication comes into play because saying you want to date doesn't mean you're ready. When your parents say, "No you can't date," you can't take it to heart because they are looking out for you. When parents shut down the dating topic it means they want you to prioritize what you're thinking about as far as your future goals. My dad did it to me multiple times. I'll have C's on my report card and not do my chores and he'll say, "Don't talk to me about dating until you can get your life prioritized." He would also say, "How can you take care of someone else if you can't take care of yourself" and he was right. If you can't take care of yourself, don't try to rush taking care of others. Taking care of yourself means getting good grades, doing your homework and chores and creating a lifestyle to succeed in life that includes setting and accomplishing goals, taking care of your mental and emotional health, and learning to invest time in interest and hobbies.

Also if you're trying to have a relationship, you need to know what you want out of it. You can't be trying to get sex because then you'll be going back to red light. You can't start a relationship then decide you don't want it because then you're confusing others because you don't know what you want. You're being indecisive and that's not healthy at all. If you don't know what you want then be single. That's the point of the yellow light time period so that you can know what you want before you get it. You wait so that you don't hurt yourself or someone else because then it won't be looking too good for you.

Last but not least, God is very important in this stage of dating because He can be heavily involved in our lives if we allow Him to be. I know for me, by writing this book, He's showing up in my life big time because He's showing me things and putting me in situations so that I can write in this book. Now I will admit I need to be more involved with God so that I know the things He wants for me on this path of life.

For me, faith in the dating world has done me well. After my ex, I didn't get into another relationship for an entire year. I decided to just wait for him to show me what girl he has for me instead of rushing it. And yes, there were times I was impatient and tried to rush things and either the girl didn't like me or didn't respond and looking back on it those were blessings in disguise.

The girls God protected me from are either now in bad relationships or are single and complain about how they are so lonely. The last girl I talked to got upset with me when I felt God tell me to slow things down. If I didn't listen to Him I wouldn't be where I am right now. I think my mentor's daughter is a reward for obeying God and finishing the project He put in my mind. First, I think this is because it wasn't that I tried to go into a relationship, her parents had to approve and evaluate me as a person let alone one to date their daughter. Second, because everything that's happening is natural. Nothing is forced and we also communicate how we feel and we understand each other's viewpoints. Her family also believes in God so we have that religious connection. I think if we tried to rush things and tried to do things our parents don't approve of then the relationship would be spoiled. There's nothing worse than trying to enjoy some food and you open it up then it spoils or it goes bad. That's what happens in a relationship when people do things that are inappropriate, the relationship goes bad and thrives off of the wrong things.

If we learn and wait to have a relationship, not only will our parents be happy, but God will also be happy with what we do. Instead of trying to date behind our parents backs, we should involve our parents in a healthy way. We should make sure our parents approve of each young woman and a young man. Also since our parents get along, it benefits our relationship as we date with flexibility and trust. As you can see having God, parent's approval and an understanding of dating will definitely benefit you in your journey on teen dating take it from me. Follow the route God has for you and you'll be surprised with where you go!

Green Light

A Female Perspective

HERE'S a story of my personal experience that ties all of what I told you together: This past year I met a guy named Brandon in September and we were friends in the beginning, as I had feelings for someone else at the time. Over the weeks relations with the other person started to fade and I spent more time with Brandon, but I still didn't quite see myself with him at the time. Brandon and I were so different in my eyes and I didn't really see us being anything more than just friends because of the friendly bond we had. I later ended things with the other guy because we didn't want the same things and my time was being wasted. Weeks passed and Brandon and I ended up getting closer as friends and feelings between us began to bud. One night we ended up telling each other how we felt and it went along the lines of "I like you but I'm not ready to be in a relationship right now." Once we communicated how we felt, we agreed to see where things would end up with us. Now, we are at the point where we want to take the next step and start a relationship together.

Ladies we are at the last stop and now is the final test to see if you are ready to pull off at the green light. My story is not to share how it should be, but show what can happen when you communicate and make smart decisions to begin a healthy relationship. Four things to learn from that story are:

- Realize what you want and if the other person doesn't want that then end it.

- Communicate how you feel, even if the other person may or may not feel the same way

- Figure out what you want your next step to be

- Notice the steps taken allows you to see a glimpse of how it can possibly work out for you.

A healthy relationship takes work, and that doesn't mean stressful work. The work you put into the relationship determines the outcome. It may seem like a lot of work, but in the end when you are in a healthy relationship it will all be worth it. Maybe right now you may say "I don't really want a relationship at the moment" and that's okay. This is not to force you into a relationship, but to inform you of the work you have to put in if a healthy relationship is something you wish to pursue in the future. As a last addition, I anonymously asked teens and young adults their idea of "what's the key to a healthy relationship" and here were some of the responses I received:

- Great communication and a deep connection
- Time
- Taking time to know and understand your partner
- Consider options; don't throw all eggs into one basket
- Learn each other's love language
- Being on the same page and having similar morals, goals, etc.

So, yes, there's more to dating than just communication, but it shows there's a lot more to focus on than just liking someone. A healthy relationship can be looked at in many different aspects, but you are the one that chooses which path you want to take. Whether you pass the green light is up to you.

QUESTIONS FOR TEENS TO THINK ABOUT

- Use the notes section to answer and think critically about what you're reading

- Think about a question(s) you would want to ask your parent(s) or trusted adult

1. Does having approval to date mean I can do whatever I want in a dating relationship? Why or why not?

2. Why would being sexually active be considered a selfish act as a teenager living at home?

3. Do you think God disapproves of dating or the behaviors demonstrated in dating that go against what He desires of those who say they're Christians?

4. Is there a difference between having friends of the opposite sex and having a boy/girlfriend if there is no sex involved? Why or why not?

5. What are three or more benefits of having your parents to talk with about dating before and while you date?

6. How can learning to talk with your parents about difficult topics and in stressful situations actually help with dating?

7. Why should you read books addressing teen related issues and learn to communicate openly with your parents?

8. What does it mean to be intelligent with life (critical thinking, decision making, problem solving)?

9. Understanding the part of the brain that involves logic, reasoning, and critical thinking doesn't fully develop until you are in your mid-twenties why then would it be helpful to include adults in how you cope with life as a teenager?

10. Why would *asking for help* be considered an essential life skill?

Notes

Conclusion

IN 2018 after breaking up with my ex-girlfriend life wasn't the best. Things were still rough because I didn't really involve my parents in my relationship. It wasn't like we were secretly seeing each other but I never communicated with my parents that this was a girl I was interested in. Not having the communication there presented problems in my relationships with my parents, especially my mom. There was constant tension between us because I wasn't communicating what was going on. Also I wasn't doing my chores and I was performing rather average in school. It showed in my grades because I was getting C's on my report card. I could do better and my parents knew I could do better. They told me there was no reason for me to date if I couldn't get my life straight. They were right and that was great advice they gave me.

When you don't talk to your parents about dating, you won't be allowed to date. They won't give you permission to do so because you're not honoring their wishes. You won't be able to date the way you want to because your parents will not be willing to cooperate with you. For the longest time my parents wouldn't even let me bring up the subject because of two scenarios. The first one being I wasn't old enough, I hadn't read my *Dateable* book and I was not performing academically to the best of my ability. Or I was old enough but I hadn't read the book and performed well enough in school. School and the book went hand in hand because those were the first priority. My age didn't really matter if I didn't read that book and did not have acceptable grades.

Before I read the book and tried to date on my own it was very hard to express my feelings. I started dating girls who were no good for me because I lusted after them for their bodies. I felt like my parents would never open up to me so I just did it on my own. Then when I did read the book but I didn't have approval from my parents, I felt a form of depression because at that time in life things were hard. I had family issues, low grades and my girlfriend and I, at the time, broke up. I felt like I was at rock bottom.

I finished reading the book in the summer of 2018; I received the book in the summer of 2014. Big difference right. That's four years of trying to make relationships work but having no guideline or instruction on how to do it. I encountered many situations that I could have avoided if I had just read the book. When I first received the book I thought it would be boring but I was optimistic about it. It was when my dad, sister and I were all in Ocean City, I had high hopes. We were challenged with reading the book on our own, and that meant I wasn't going to read. When I was in 8th grade I didn't feel like it was worth it, my friends thought it was lame and so did I eventually. I ended up losing the book in my room after paying no attention to it. Reading the book in general benefitted me because it taught me more about myself. It also put me in a position where I didn't have to deal with the things my friends had to deal with because reading the book saved me from avoidable mistakes. Therefore, you need to learn about yourself before you can learn about someone else. Learning about yourself and investing in yourself benefits you when you date because you know more about what you're getting into.

Self-investing isn't just about putting money into yourself. It can be money but it can also be time such as reading or exercising or trying new things to see what you like. This isn't just an important step in starting a relationship, it's an important part in self-development. New experiences help you grow as a person. Another important aspect of life is having a strong relationship with Jesus Christ. God will lead you to do many great things in your life such as writing books, public speaking or using your talent to benefit you or others in a positive way to give him glory. If you try to get in the way and control that, then you won't make it very far in life the way he desires you to. In my dating life, journaling, prayer and bible reading helped me become a more positive person. I did it for a while when I was in my last relationship and I felt more joyful and positive whenever I did so. I feel that everyone should do these things to become closer to God. God wants us to connect with Him and make a strong connection so that we can talk to Him. Talking to God is praying in its simplest form. Journaling is praying as well, because you are writing on paper your thoughts to God. You may feel like that helps more but I did both. But most importantly reading the Bible is what God wants from us. It's the instruction manual of life. The Bible makes life easier because you know how to operate with the power of God in your life. These three things won't just change your dating life, they will change your life in general.

God has already made a plan for you and in that plan He puts the things you will benefit from. So if a girlfriend or boyfriend is not in the plan don't worry about it. Don't force something into your life that doesn't need to be there. I've learned that if God hasn't given you something then you're not ready for it or it's because He has something better planned for you. Just like the prodigal son in the Bible. He wanted his inheritance too soon because he wasn't supposed to get it until his father passed but he couldn't wait. So his father gave him what he asked for even though he wasn't deserving or ready for it. Without having any knowledge on how to manage his money he wasted it and became poor. He looked back at what he did and went back home. His father welcomed him back with open arms and threw him a party because he was happy his son returned home.

Now you're thinking what does that have to do with dating? The inheritance he demanded was supposed to be given to him later in life. He's being selfish, inconsiderate, and impatient. The inheritance in the story is your opportunity to do in the future, what you desire with parental approval or when you become an adult. The father in the story represents God just like our parents represent God in the story. God desires for us to be patient. If you decide to date behind your parents back then you are making the same decision, as the prodigal son demanded his inheritance. Impatience in desiring to date leads to sex, lack of trust from parents and you end up being disappointed more often. You waste your time doing things you don't need to do. Then you begin to wander looking for the wrong things as you lose your parents trust and the burden of guilt begins to eat away at you. You start to feel alone, isolated without perspective and guidance. God wants you to avoid all of that. God wants you to wait and He wants you to learn what you're doing before you waste your time and energy in things that don't benefit you. So be smart and don't date too soon or else you'll be dealing with things that were avoidable. God wants you to be safe and secure in yourself in being single. Dating does not provide that, this is what your parents are trying to protect you from.

Last but not least is time management. It's a life skill that you learn how to manage your time. Time is all we have and if you waste it you'll be out of it when you need it. A great way to manage your time is to create a calendar. Creating a calendar gives you a layout of time and the days you can do things. You can open a calendar on your phone with Google. It helps you stay on track with what you have to get done. Looking back on life, waiting a full year to start getting back into dating really benefited me. It wasn't that I wanted to wait, it just happened. God played a major part in that though because He gave me the idea of writing this book after I read the book, *Dateable* in 2018. Then I had a year and a half worth of life to put into a piece of art I can use to help make the world a better place and help youth learn about what they are getting into.

After reading the book and finishing my own, I can definitely say life has changed for me in ways I didn't think it would a year and a half ago. My family life is amazing. My relationship with my mom is great and will continue to get better. My grades are good. I finished the first quarter of my senior year with a 3.45 GPA. I feel joy and I feel mentally prepared to deal with whatever relationship I deal with. God took control of my life and did things that I never would have thought could happen. God has shaped me into the person I am today.

Dating the right way helped me get to where I am now. Following God's plan for my life got me to where I am now. God does nothing by mistake. Everything He does in your life is on purpose so let Him do his thing. Don't try to control God, let God do His work and you'll be surprised with what you get.

www.ingramcontent.com/pod-product-compliance
Lightning Source LLC
Chambersburg PA
CBHW030302030426
42336CB00009B/489